JAZZ PLAY ALONG

Book and CD for B♭, E♭ and C Instruments

Arranged and Produced by Mark Taylor

Volume 28

BIG BAND ERA
10 BIG BAND FAVORITES

T0053208

ISBN 978-0-634-06831-7

HAL•LEONARD®
CORPORATION

7777 W. BLUEMOUND RD. P.O. BOX 13819 MILWAUKEE, WI 53213

Visit Hal Leonard Online at
www.halleonard.com

BIG BAND ERA

Arranged and Produced by
Mark Taylor

Featured Players:

Graham Breedlove-Trumpet
John Desalme-Tenor Sax
Tony Nalker-Piano
Jim Roberts and Paul Henry-Bass
Steve Fidyk-Drums

Recorded at Bias Studios, Springfield, Virginia
Bob Dawson, Engineer

HOW TO USE THE CD:

Each song has <u>two</u> tracks:

1) Split Track/Melody

Woodwind, Brass, Keyboard, and **Mallet Players** can use this track as a learning tool for melody, style and inflection.

Bass Players can learn and perform with this track – remove the recorded bass track by turning down the volume on the LEFT channel.

Keyboard and **Guitar Players** can learn and perform with this track – remove the recorded piano part by turning down the volume on the RIGHT channel.

2) Full Stereo Track

Soloists or **Groups** can learn and perform with this accompaniment track with the RHYTHM SECTION only.

OPUS ONE

WORDS AND MUSIC BY
SY OLIVER

❶ : SPLIT TRACK/MELODY
❷ : FULL STEREO TRACK

C VERSION

3: SPLIT TRACK/MELODY
4: FULL STEREO TRACK

C VERSION

Tuxedo Junction

WORDS BY BUDDY FEYNE
MUSIC BY ERSKINE HAWKINS,
WILLIAM JOHNSON, AND JULIAN DASH

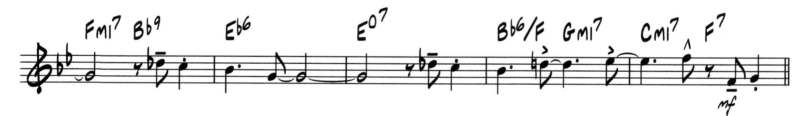

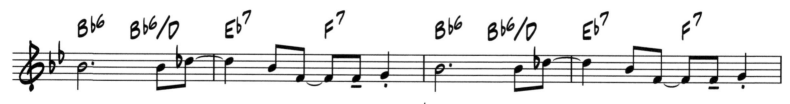

CHRISTOPHER COLUMBUS

5 : SPLIT TRACK/MELODY
6 : FULL STEREO TRACK

C VERSION

LYRIC BY ANDY RAZAF
MUSIC BY LEON BERRY

SWING

mf (PLAY WITH BASS)

f (LEAD)

7 : SPLIT TRACK/MELODY
8 : FULL STEREO TRACK

C VERSION

IN THE MOOD

MUSIC BY JOE GARLAND

(PLAY AS WRITTEN 2ND TIME ONLY)

4 TIMES (PLAY 8VA LAST TIME)

INTERMISSION RIFF

9 : SPLIT TRACK/MELODY
10 : FULL STEREO TRACK

C VERSION

MUSIC BY RAY WETZEL
WORDS BY STEVE GRAHAM

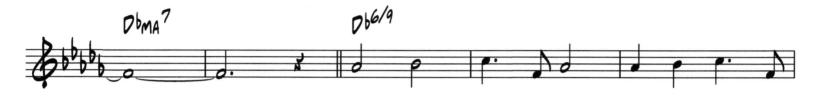

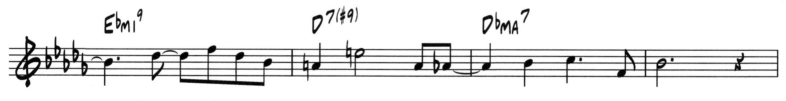

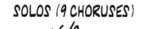

Jersey Bounce

WORDS BY ROBERT WRIGHT
MUSIC BY BOBBY PLATTER, TINY BRADSHAW,
ED JOHNSON AND ROBERT WRIGHT

CD
⓫: SPLIT TRACK/MELODY
⓬: FULL STEREO TRACK

C VERSION

A String of Pearls

13 : SPLIT TRACK/MELODY
14 : FULL STEREO TRACK

C VERSION

MUSIC BY JERRY GRAY

FOUR BROTHERS

C VERSION

MUSIC BY JIMMY GUIFFRE

SOLOS (3 CHORUSES)

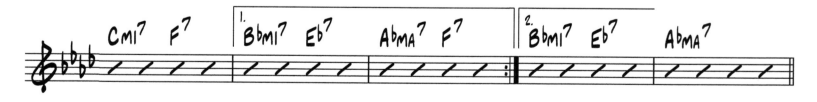

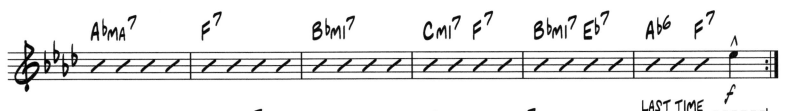

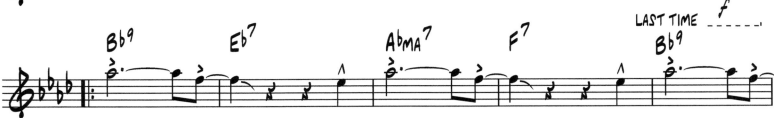

17 : SPLIT TRACK/MELODY
18 : FULL STEREO TRACK

C VERSION

STOMPIN' AT THE SAVOY

MUSIC BY BENNY GOODMAN,
EDGAR SAMPSON AND CHICK WEBB

SOLOS (2 CHORUSES)

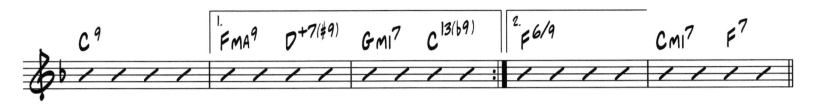

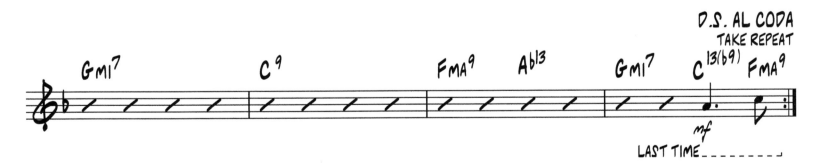

D.S. AL CODA
TAKE REPEAT

LAST TIME

CODA

AIR MAIL SPECIAL

MUSIC BY BENNY GOODMAN,
JIMMY MUNDY, AND CHARLIE CHRISTIAN

SOLOS (4 CHORUSES)

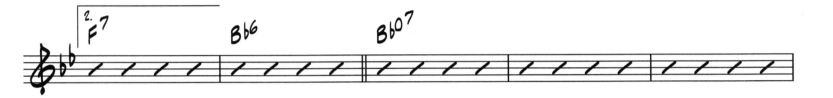

D.S. AL CODA
(TAKE REPEAT)

PIANO
LAST TIME

OPUS ONE

Bb VERSION

WORDS AND MUSIC BY
SY OLIVER

SOLOS (2 CHORUSES)

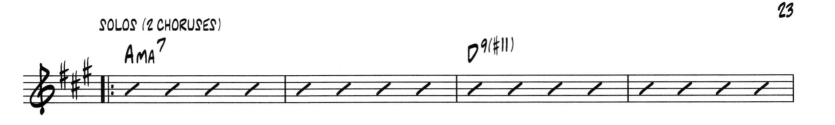

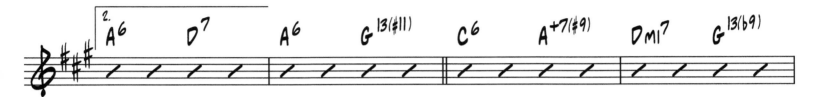

D.S. AL CODA
TAKE REPEAT

Tuxedo Junction

WORDS BY BUDDY FEYNE
MUSIC BY ERSKINE HAWKINS,
WILLIAM JOHNSON, AND JULIAN DASH

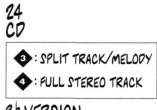

◆③: SPLIT TRACK/MELODY
◆④: FULL STEREO TRACK

B♭ Version

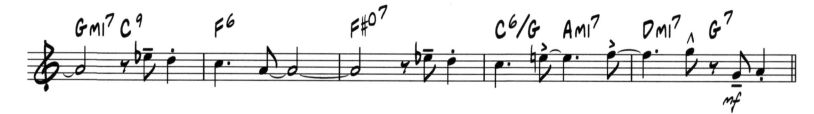

CHRISTOPHER COLUMBUS

LYRIC BY ANDY RAZAF
MUSIC BY LEON BERRY

SWING

mf (PLAY WITH BASS)

f (LEAD)

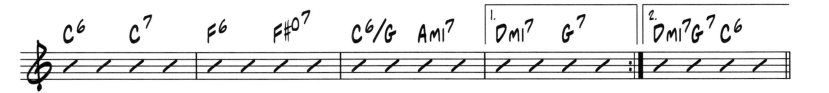

In the Mood

MUSIC BY JOE GARLAND

♦7: SPLIT TRACK/MELODY
♦8: FULL STEREO TRACK

B♭ VERSION

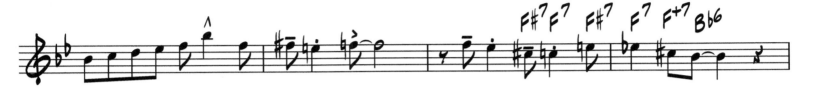

(PLAY AS WRITTEN 2ND TIME ONLY)

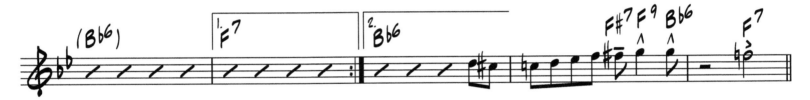

4 TIMES (OPT. 8VA LAST TIME)

9: SPLIT TRACK/MELODY
10: FULL STEREO TRACK

Bb VERSION

INTERMISSION RIFF

MUSIC BY RAY WETZEL
WORDS BY STEVE GRAHAM

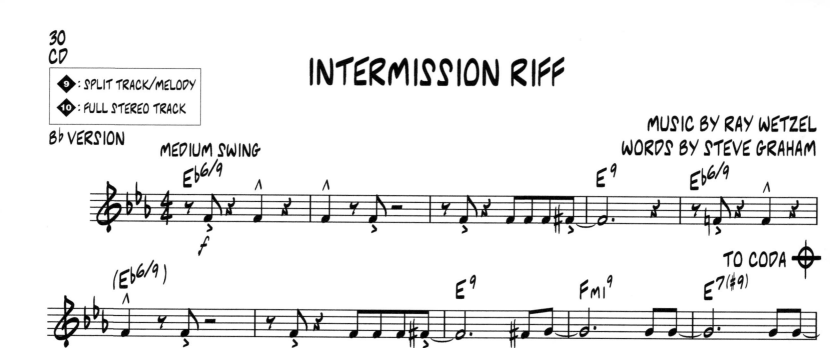

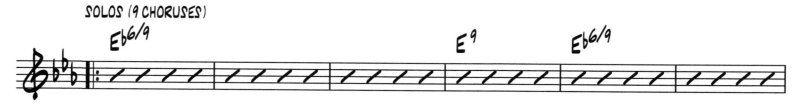

Jersey Bounce

CD
□11: SPLIT TRACK/MELODY
□12: FULL STEREO TRACK

Bb VERSION

WORDS BY ROBERT WRIGHT
MUSIC BY BOBBY PLATTER, TINY BRADSHAW,
ED JOHNSON AND ROBERT WRIGHT

A String of Pearls

Bb Version

MUSIC BY JERRY GRAY

SOLOS (5 CHORUSES)

1ST TIME ONLY - - -

LAST TIME _____ RHYTHM _____

PIANO

PIANO

15 : SPLIT TRACK/MELODY
16 : FULL STEREO TRACK

FOUR BROTHERS

Bb VERSION   FAST SWING

MUSIC BY JIMMY GUIFFRE

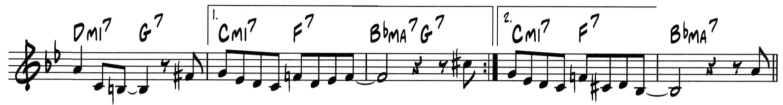

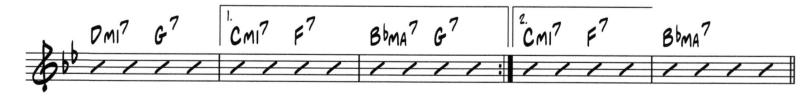

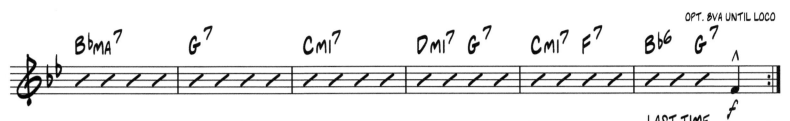

17 : SPLIT TRACK/MELODY
18 : FULL STEREO TRACK

Bb VERSION

STOMPIN' AT THE SAVOY

MUSIC BY BENNY GOODMAN,
EDGAR SAMPSON AND CHICK WEBB

SOLOS (2 CHORUSES)

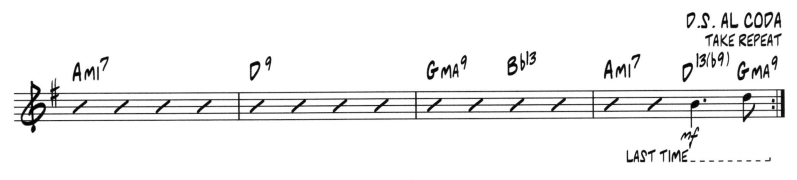

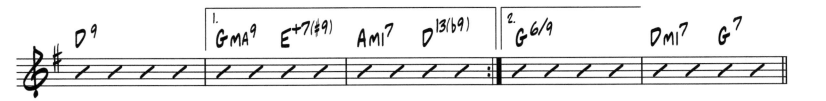

D.S. AL CODA
TAKE REPEAT

LAST TIME _ _ _ _ _ _ _ _

Air Mail Special

MUSIC BY BENNY GOODMAN,
JIMMY MUNDY, AND CHARLIE CHRISTIAN

Bb VERSION

SOLOS (4 CHORUSES)

OPUS ONE

Eb VERSION

WORDS AND MUSIC BY
SY OLIVER

FAST SWING

TO CODA ⊕

SOLOS (2 CHORUSES)

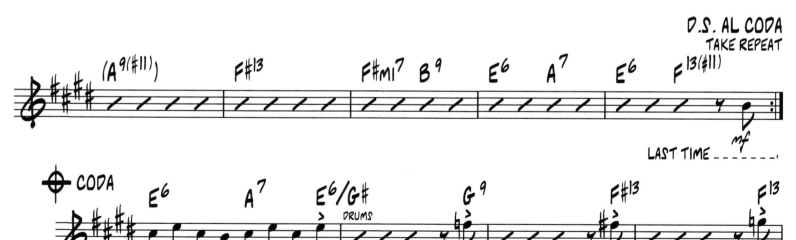

Tuxedo Junction

③: SPLIT TRACK/MELODY
④: FULL STEREO TRACK

E♭ VERSION

WORDS BY BUDDY FEYNE
MUSIC BY ERSKINE HAWKINS,
WILLIAM JOHNSON, AND JULIAN DASH

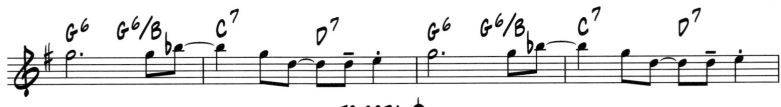

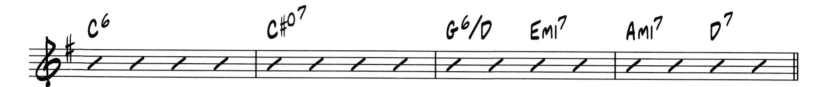

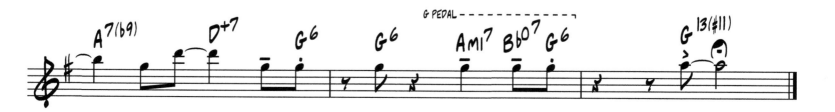

5 : SPLIT TRACK/MELODY
6 : FULL STEREO TRACK

Eb VERSION

CHRISTOPHER COLUMBUS

LYRIC BY ANDY RAZAF
MUSIC BY LEON BERRY

FINE

SOLOS (3 CHORUSES)

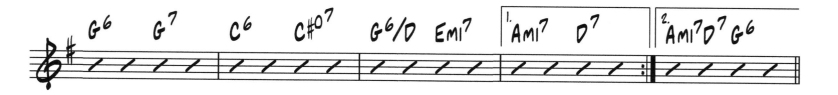

D.C. AL FINE
(LAST TIME)

7 : SPLIT TRACK/MELODY
8 : FULL STEREO TRACK

Eb VERSION

IN THE MOOD

MUSIC BY JOE GARLAND

(PLAY AS WRITTEN 2ND TIME ONLY)

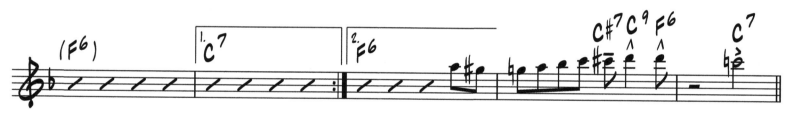

4 TIMES (OPT. 8VA LAST TIME)

INTERMISSION RIFF

MUSIC BY RAY WETZEL
WORDS BY STEVE GRAHAM

Eb VERSION   MEDIUM SWING

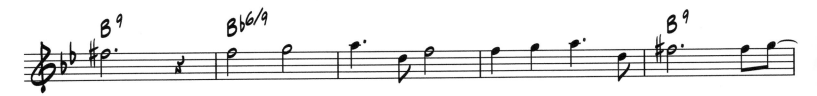

Jersey Bounce

WORDS BY ROBERT WRIGHT
MUSIC BY BOBBY PLATTER, TINY BRADSHAW,
ED JOHNSON AND ROBERT WRIGHT

CD
11: SPLIT TRACK/MELODY
12: FULL STEREO TRACK

Eb VERSION

A String of Pearls

13: SPLIT TRACK/MELODY
14: FULL STEREO TRACK

Eb Version

Medium Swing

MUSIC BY JERRY GRAY

SOLOS (5 CHORUSES)

F6   Bb7   F6   F7

1ST TIME ONLY - - -

Bb7   F6

C7   F6   (E9)

LAST TIME   RHYTHM

A Ama7 A7 A6 A+ A A+ A6 A7 Ama7 A Ama7

mf

A7 A6 A+ A B9 E7 A6 B7(b9) E9

PIANO

A Ama7 A7 A6 A+ A A+ A6 A7 Ama7 A Ama7

A7 A6 A+ A B9 E7 A6 Bmi7/F# E°7 D6 C#°7 Bmi7 F9 E13

E13 A6/9 A6/9

PIANO

FOUR BROTHERS

Eb VERSION   FAST SWING

MUSIC BY JIMMY GUIFFRE

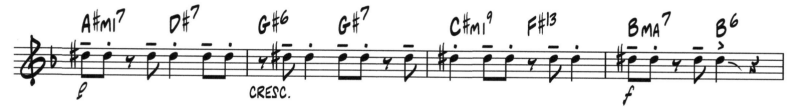

STOMPIN' AT THE SAVOY

17: SPLIT TRACK/MELODY
18: FULL STEREO TRACK

Eb VERSION

MUSIC BY BENNY GOODMAN,
EDGAR SAMPSON AND CHICK WEBB

MEDIUM SWING

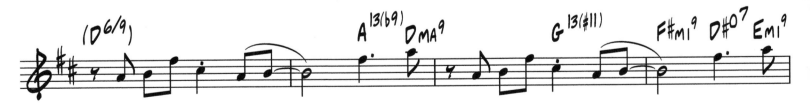

SOLOS (2 CHORUSES)

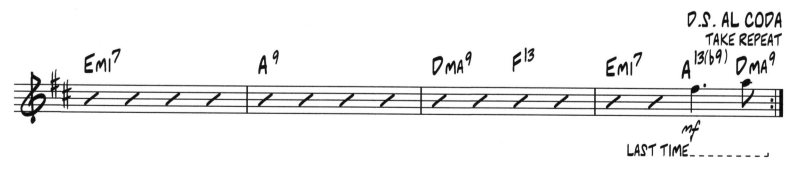

19: SPLIT TRACK/MELODY
20: FULL STEREO TRACK

Eb VERSION

AIR MAIL SPECIAL

MUSIC BY BENNY GOODMAN,
JIMMY MUNDY, AND CHARLIE CHRISTIAN

OPUS ONE

WORDS AND MUSIC BY
SY OLIVER

❶: SPLIT TRACK/MELODY
❷: FULL STEREO TRACK

𝄢: C VERSION

SOLOS (2 CHORUSES)

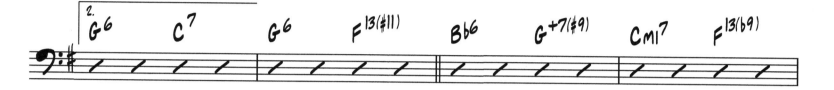

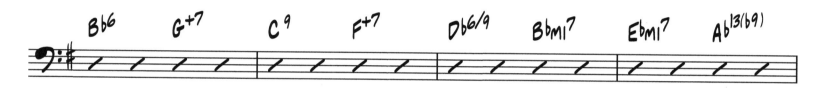

Tuxedo Junction

WORDS BY BUDDY FEYNE
MUSIC BY ERSKINE HAWKINS,
WILLIAM JOHNSON, AND JULIAN DASH

③ : SPLIT TRACK/MELODY
④ : FULL STEREO TRACK

♪: C VERSION

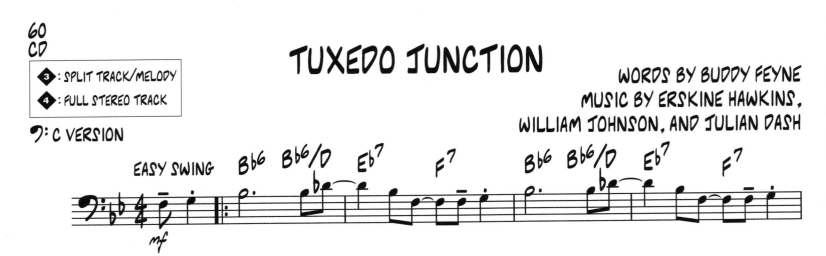

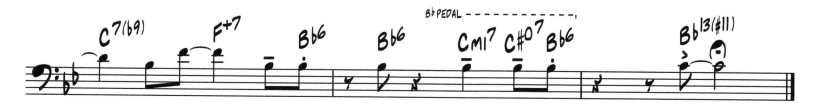

CHRISTOPHER COLUMBUS

LYRIC BY ANDY RAZAF
MUSIC BY LEON BERRY

𝄢: C VERSION

FINE

SOLOS (3 CHORUSES)

D.C. AL FINE
(LAST TIME)

IN THE MOOD

7: SPLIT TRACK/MELODY
8: FULL STEREO TRACK

7: C VERSION

MUSIC BY JOE GARLAND

INTERMISSION RIFF

MUSIC BY RAY WETZEL
WORDS BY STEVE GRAHAM

♦ : SPLIT TRACK/MELODY
◊ : FULL STEREO TRACK

𝄢: C VERSION

MEDIUM SWING

SOLOS (9 CHORUSES)

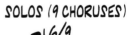

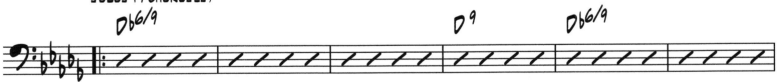

Jersey Bounce

WORDS BY ROBERT WRIGHT
MUSIC BY BOBBY PLATTER, TINY BRADSHAW,
ED JOHNSON AND ROBERT WRIGHT

A String of Pearls

MUSIC BY JERRY GRAY

𝄢: C VERSION   MEDIUM SWING

FOUR BROTHERS

MUSIC BY JIMMY GUIFFRE

🎼: C VERSION

OPT. 8VA TO LOCO

LAST TIME _____ _f_____

CRESC.   _f_

_mf_   CRESC.   _ff_

STOMPIN' AT THE SAVOY

17: SPLIT TRACK/MELODY
18: FULL STEREO TRACK

MUSIC BY BENNY GOODMAN,
EDGAR SAMPSON AND CHICK WEBB

𝄢 : C VERSION

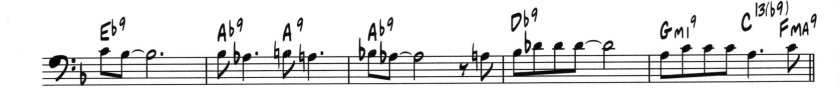

SOLOS (2 CHORUSES)

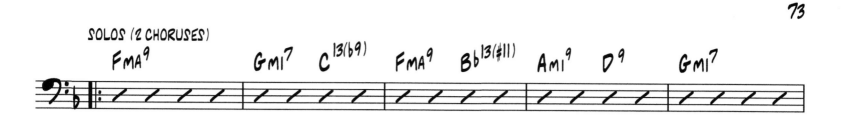

D.S. AL CODA
TAKE REPEAT

LAST TIME _ _ _ _ _ _ _ _ _

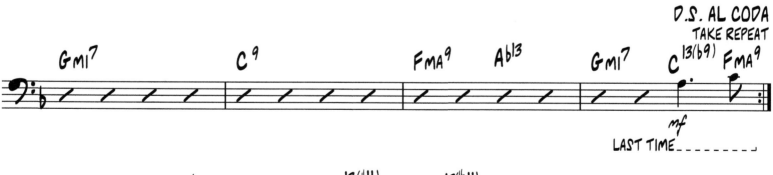

AIR MAIL SPECIAL

**MUSIC BY BENNY GOODMAN,
JIMMY MUNDY, AND CHARLIE CHRISTIAN**

19 : SPLIT TRACK/MELODY
20 : FULL STEREO TRACK

🎵: C VERSION

SOLOS (4 CHORUSES)

D.S. AL CODA
(TAKE REPEAT)

PIANO
LAST TIME _ _ _ _ _ _ _

CODA
(Bb6)

Presenting the Hal Leonard JAZZ PLAY-ALONG® SERIES

Prices, contents, and availability subject to change without notice.

FOR MORE INFORMATION,
SEE YOUR LOCAL MUSIC DEALER,
OR WRITE TO:

HAL•LEONARD®
CORPORATION
7777 W. BLUEMOUND RD. P.O. BOX 13819
MILWAUKEE, WISCONSIN 53213

Visit Hal Leonard online at
www.halleonard.com
for complete songlists.

0910